Flashes of FedEx

By

Brenda Copeland

Other Books by Brenda Copeland:

The Doll in the Blue Velvet Dress

A delightful Christmas Story

COMING SOON

OVERTIME

A psychological thriller set in a
major corporation. A must-read!

FREEPORT FOREVER – Growing up in
Freeport, Bahamas – the Boomtown
Years.

Available at
https://www.createspace.com/3562284

Amazon.com, Kindle

Facebook Brenda Smith Copeland

Brendacopeland3@aol.com

This book is dedicated with love and admiration to my fabulous sisters, Pam, Carole, Linda and Debbie, and to my cool brother Gary.

And to my parents, A.R. and Gloria Smith, who gave me the love of flying . . .

Chapter 1

JUMP SEAT

The wind was whipping my hair all over my face that cold October night as I walked up the ramp and stopped at the open door of the Federal Express cargo jet. I was happy to finally be at the airplane because I had just spent over two hours awaiting this flight in the doublewide trailer that served FedEx jump seaters.

A jump seater is a person who rides on an airplane in one of the extra seats called jump seats. Jump seats are usually inside of the cockpit and/or just outside of the cockpit door of most commercial airplanes.

To me one of the greatest benefits of working for FedEx was that the company allowed its employees to ride jump seat in its jets. FedEx flies all over the world! My family and friends are scattered, so free flight gave me a way to truly keep in touch. Plus, I loved to travel and probably would have worked for FedEx for free just to get the flight benefits.

Besides offering jump seat benefits, Federal Express offers flight discounts on commercial airlines. If an employee preferred, he or she could fly commercially at a discount instead of flying jump seat. I have heard employees say they would rather buy a discounted commercial ticket rather than bother with the late night hours and discomfort of jump seating. I saw things differently.

My view is that jump seating is more exciting than flying commercially. Anyone can buy a commercial plane ticket, but very few people have the privilege of flying jump seat.

I loved the idea of being in the thick of things by riding in the jump seat of a FedEx jet in the middle of the night, along with all of those urgent packages. Packages that people all over the world, were eager to receive.

FedEx holds the view that every package is what's called the 'Golden Package.' You never know how very important any package is so you assume that it is of the highest importance to someone and you treat it as such by helping it to move through the system until it reaches its destination, on time and intact.

I've heard comments from people who know that I worked for FedEx about their Golden package. One was simply a package of homemade cookies sent at great expense to a lonely, homesick college student. Another was an engagement ring, safely received in time for a proposal.

And yet another, the most Golden one of all, was when a mother received a gift from her daughter on Mother's Day. That Mother's Day turned out to be her last, and her daughter was so thankful that her gift had arrived on time.

And, here I was, about to ride the jump seat on one of Federal Express' jets along with all of those Golden packages.

Checking in at Jump Seat had been easy. I simply showed my ticket as well as my employee ID to a Jump Seat agent.

"Ms. Copeland, just take a seat and wait for your flight to be called. It's flight 248 to Atlanta. Once it's called, just leave through that door." he said as he pointed to a door behind the check-in desk.

"You will see a white van. That's the shuttle and it will take you to your flight. You're good to go. Have a safe flight."

He started helping the next jump seater in line. I looked around for a place to wait. There were various types of chairs, including a couple of recliners that were in a dim corner. I claimed one of those for myself. The recliner was soft and comfortable. In a few minutes my eyelids began to droop. Despite drinking a hot cup of coffee on the moonlit drive to Jump Seat, I felt drowsy.

Now that I was in the comfy recliner, I was in real danger of immediately falling asleep. Since I didn't want to risk missing my flight announcement, I moved to a less comfortable chair in a well-lighted area of the room.

Once I changed seats, I looked around for things to do to keep my mind occupied so I wouldn't get sleepy again. I saw that travel posters were on the walls and I looked at them to help pass the time.

Most of the posters depicted various major cities. One showed La Tour Eiffel, the Eiffel Tower. I had never been to Paris, but it was on my bucket list. My great grandmother spoke French, and I had a natural affinity for all things French.

I looked at another poster. It showed a close up of a cowboy boot in the stirrup of a Western saddle. The saddle was on a black horse. The word 'Dallas' was in large print near the bottom of the poster.

Since I was born in Dallas and like horses, I liked that poster the most.

Besides looking at posters to pass the time, I reflected on my being hired by Federal Express as a permanent employee six months previously. Just prior to being hired by FedEx, I had been working for an agency that supplied temporary employees to various companies. The company I was assigned to before getting on with FedEx was a successful property developer. This property developer built outlet malls and many other commercial income properties.

Their corporate offices were luxuriously appointed. The office supplies are kept in antique armoires, visitors sit in vintage leather wingback chairs, and the conference room table looks as though it came from the dining hall of a castle. I really appreciate fine things, and could have easily worked permanently for this company.

But one day while working at my desk, occasionally sipping tea from my English bone china cup, I looked up to see the head of

Personnel for the company standing before me. "Brenda, would you mind coming to my office?"

Now, I don't know about you, but when anyone asks me to come to his office, I feel as though I'm in trouble. I must have a serious guilt complex, or the times I was called into the office in high school for some infraction has scarred me for life. I attended a British high school, which had strict rules on things that an American school would not have a problem with.

I was reprimanded for not having my hair 'up.' I received detention for walking under the flagpole, and I got detention for laughing in detention. What a juvenile delinquent I was!

As I walked behind him, my mind played

different scenarios as to why he wanted me in his office. Maybe he wanted to hire me. As a temporary employee, any job offers are usually handled via the Temporary Agency rather than directly through a company to which the temporary employee is sent. So that couldn't be it.

Maybe he wasn't happy with me and was going to let me go. But again, that would have been handled through my employment agency.

I followed the manager into his office.

He pointed towards a red, deeply-tufted Chesterfield sofa.

"Have a seat."

I sat down and faced his desk. I was wearing a black top and matching skirt with embossed bamboo in the pattern and black patent leather high heels. And, although I usually wear my hair loose, today I had my hair up, with two chopsticks holding it. Maybe he didn't like the look. I wasn't quite sure of it myself.

He walked around to his chair and sat down. "I'm sure you're wondering why I called you in here."

"Yes, I am." I answered.

"I have been told by a member of this company that they are very pleased with your work." he said. Then he added "And he wanted me to ask you if you would like to come to work for us as a permanent employee?"

I immediately felt relieved that they were pleased with my work. And, although I knew that the company was a good fit for me, when the moment came to make a decision, I never hesitated with my answer.

"As tempting as your offer is, it wouldn't be fair to you for me to accept it as I am trying to get on with Federal Express."

He didn't seem surprised. He was probably aware of the saying in Memphis that there are only two kinds of people, those who work for Federal Express, and those who want to work for Federal Express.

"Well, I understand. But if you ever change your mind, we would be glad to have you work for us."

Back at my desk, I thought about why I wanted to work for Federal Express. I knew I wanted to work for a company with a world-wide reach, flight benefits, and which gave the feeling that *anything* was possible. I wanted to be part of a company that had a 'boomtown' atmosphere.

I was raised in a boomtown, Freeport, Bahamas. The atmosphere in Freeport was one of tremendous excitement as businesses, private homes or beautiful parks went up. Movie stars roamed the hotels and beaches. Princess Grace of Monaco visited. The world's largest Holiday Inn went up. A sunken treasure was discovered one mile off the beach. You had the feeling that anything wonderful and worthwhile was possible in Freeport.

Freeport was founded by Wallace Groves, an entrepreneur from Virginia. He was a genius who earned four degrees at Georgetown University in four years and a building is named in his honor there. Groves commanded respect and because of his cachet, businesses sprang up in Freeport almost as fast as buildings could be built to house them.

I worked as a computer programmer at Island Data Processing in Freeport. It was not possible for me to be any happier. But boomtowns have a way of going bust. After Mr. Groves left the leadership of Freeport, and it went independent from England, things went downhill as fast as they had boomed before.

Many thousands of people lost their jobs, including myself. I left my job, and worse, my beloved island home, and headed for Memphis, TN. I landed in Memphis, not quite on my feet, and was met with major culture shock.

It's hard to go from an island where people from every socio-economic background are friendly and speak to you. We spoke in stores, at church, from table to table at restaurants, on the beach, at the stable, well, anywhere we met. We invited strangers to leave their hotels and stay at our home. If there were a party going on, we pulled up and went in, no invitation required.

The feeling of anonymity in this big American city was almost unbearable to me. I felt terribly isolated and invisible. I learned what the term, 'the silence is deafening,' really meant.

I continued to speak to people, even if they almost never answered. I was like Crocodile Dundee in New York City, talking to New Yorkers who were shocked by his interest in talking to them. I remember one time, I said good morning to a girl in the hallway at Memphis State. She actually crossed the hall to avoid me as though I were some sort of perp.

She may have thought of me as a perp, but honestly, I thought of her as a Zombie. I couldn't imagine walking past someone, especially someone about your age, same sex, dressed neatly, and not acknowledging them in some way.

Anyway, back to the job at hand; I had to find a job, and I had to start from square one, if not minus square one. I basically took any job close to where I lived, no matter the hours or pay. I had no connections in Memphis, and really just didn't have a clue as to how to go about getting a 'real' job in a big city.

Eventually the buzz started in Memphis about a start-up company that delivered packages overnight, and that offered flight benefits. It sounded like the kind of work place I was hoping for. I began mailing resumes to the company. This went on for years with no response, not even a rejection letter. Over the years, without even realizing it, I gradually became accustomed to the thought that getting on at Federal Express was impossible.

This job offer reminded me that I really didn't want to settle, no matter how good another company was. I decided to refocus on my goal of getting hired by Federal Express.

But *how* would I get on with Federal Express? I had heard from a friend who worked there that the company got over *one hundred thousand* resumes per week. I knew that my resume would never be noticed with so much competition. It was time to take a different tack.

At that moment I realized that I must get *inside* of Federal Express, and then try for a permanent job.

I figured that Federal Express must use temporary employees. So, in the next few days, I asked around and learned which temporary employment agency provided employees for Federal Express. When I found the agency I was looking for, I applied to work for that agency.

To my delight, I was immediately assigned to Federal Express! I was to report to FedEx the following Monday morning at 8:00 a.m.

The Saturday before I was to be on the job, I did a dry run, driving the 70-mile round trip from my home to the address on my assignment voucher. I made this trip to lessen my anxiety when I actually had to be at the address. Sometimes there are obstacles such as train tracks or road construction that could slow me down, and I wanted to ensure that I knew about them so that I wouldn't be late.

The following Monday, I was on time at the address specified. A young woman I'll call 'K' greeted me in the lobby of the building that housed some Federal Express offices. The company was growing so fast that buildings all over Memphis, especially near the airport, burgeoned with various divisions of the company.

K escorted me to an elevator, where we were whisked up to the third floor. When the doors opened, I stepped into a Federal Express office. At last, my high-heeled foot was in the door.

There were cubicles everywhere in the center of the room, and offices were along the outside walls. People were working at their desks, or walking with files or mugs of coffee in their hands.

K announced "Everybody, this is Brenda Copeland. She'll be covering for Marty this week."

People looked up and said "Hi" and "Welcome Brenda."

Someone said, "I Hope we don't run you off."

"Not a chance." I answered.

"Our receptionist is on vacation." K said. "We'll just need you to answer phones." she explained. "The break room is across the hall and the lady's room is just around the corner," she said as she pointed to an area across the room.

K walked me over to a reception desk. The wall behind the desk sported the words in shiny metal 'Business Service Centers.' Most people are familiar with the Business Service Centers that are in every town in America and in many locations around the world, but at that time, I had never heard of them.

"Just answer the phone, 'Federal Express, BSC Division, Brenda speaking.'"

'Simple enough.' I thought.

"When you take a message, put it up in one of these slots. They're in alphabetical order, and everyone on this floor has one."

No problem," I answered. "And, just so you know," I added, "I'm proficient at MS Word and Excel, if you need me to help out."

"I'll keep that in mind," K said, before she left me to my tasks.

I looked around the room. The walls and

carpeting were soft mauve, and the essential office items such as desks, desk sets, telephones, file cabinets, and swivel chairs all appeared to be fairly new.

As people dropped by to check on their messages, they introduced themselves, picked up their messages, and headed to their respective areas.

Most women wore dresses and high heels and the men wore business suits and ties. Each had his Federal Express ID badge clipped to his clothes where it could easily been seen, usually on a jacket lapel or the edge of a pocket.

There was a printer on the credenza behind my chair. I looked at the letterhead paper in the printer. It had a purple slash across the top left-hand side and the address of the corporate office.

I hoped to get an offer letter one day on that letterhead as I was still a 'Temp'.

By the end of my five days, I was asked to come back to do some secretarial work in the Personnel Office of the Business Service Center Division. My five days turned into ten months of working non-stop as a temporary employee in the BSC Division.

Then, one day, K came over to my desk. "Brenda, Marcy is moving up, and the receptionist position will be advertised next week. I thought I'd offer it to you, if you're interested." (I don't know . . . let me think about it . . .) I accepted the job! After a flurry of paperwork and picture-taking, I proudly clipped my ID Badge, still warm from the laminating machine, to my jacket. It was official. I was employee 35539 - a permanent FedEx employee! *F-I-N-A-L-L-Y!*

I immersed myself in the New-Hire manual that I had been provided. One benefit that appealed to me was tuition reimbursement. I knew I would take advantage of that.

A month after I started working as a receptionist, I moved up to a secretarial position in BSC Personnel. They hired another temporary employee to answer phones.

Since I worked in BSC Personnel, the first thing I did after being hired was to take two of my sisters' resumes to the Director of Human Resources for the BSC division. Both of my sisters were hired by the Company as Customer Service Representatives.

The second thing I did after getting on with Federal Express was to find out how long it would be before I became eligible to fly on jump seat. I am a person who dearly loves to fly, and after a long drought of flightlessness, this human Dodo bird could hardly wait until she could fly with Federal Express.

I found that I would be eligible to fly on a Federal Express jump seat six months from my date of hire. Since I was hired in May, I calculated that I would be eligible to jump seat in October of that year.

The clock went Tick . . .

Tock . . .

Tick . . .

Tock . . . until October *finally* arrived.   I was eligible to jump seat!

Not so fast though.

Flying in the cockpit of a jet has its serious side and an employee cannot ride jump seat until they are approved to do so.   In order to be approved to ride jump seat, an employee must pass the Jump Seat Accreditation test, which they can prepare for by studying the Jump Seat manual.

Both the manual and the test are online so it is easy for employees to access them.

I studied the manual at my desk. The manual went over safety procedures while onboard the various types of jets that Federal Express flies.

One procedure showed how to exit the plane in case of emergency. I learned that I could exit through the cabin door or even through a side cockpit window (backside first). Another procedure outlined how to activate the emergency slide, which can also be used as a raft. By the time I was eligible to fly jump seat, I was quite prepared to take the test.

I signed in to the Jump Seat Accreditation test from my work computer. It was easy to complete and I completed the test satisfactorily.

The system then gave me the option to choose a location to which I wanted to fly. Since I wanted to visit another of my sisters, who lives in Atlanta, I selected Atlanta. I then printed a round trip ticket to Atlanta.

Now, here at Jump Seat, I opened my purse and double checked my single-sheet ticket to make sure I had it before my flight was called. It was still in my purse, so I sighed with relief and continued the tedious process of waiting. The flights started after one a.m. and my flight was closer to two a.m.

I continued to wait. And wait. . .

"Denver, we're rollin'." suddenly blared over the intercom.

Then, "Where's my jump seater for Chicago?"

Pilots were calling for their jump seaters. I sat up and listened carefully.

More calls for jump seaters.

"Jump seater for Austin,

"Newark, "

"Ft. Lauderdale,"

"And a woman's voice, "280 to Mobile."

More men's voices, "Flight 233, Cleveland,"

"1295 to Newark,"

Then, "Flight 248, to Atlanta."

"That's me!" I thought. I stood up, picked up my carry on and walked quickly towards the

Exit door which was just past the Jump Seat Check-In console. I walked out of the building into the cool October night air. I immediately saw the white van that I had been told to look for. Several people including pilots were boarding the van, and I boarded it too. It felt good to be on the van, one step closer to my eagerly awaited experience of flying Jump Seat.

The van pulled away from the sidewalk, and headed down a long straightaway. Federal Express jets were lined up on the right of this straightaway like enormous race horses posed to leap from the starting gate. The van stopped at each jet where the driver announced the destination for each jet. People exited the van if that plane was going to their destination. The van stopped at a jet, and the driver announced: "Flight 248 to Atlanta."

I stood up from my seat and walked to the front. Since no one else got up from his seat, I realized that I would probably be the only jump seater on the flight. I thanked the driver and stepped off the van into the cold October night.

Once I exited the van, I stopped and looked around me. The hustle and bustle that met my eyes looked like a scene from a sci-fi movie. Numerous people, dressed in dark blue uniforms and wearing ear protection, were working in an efficient ant-like manner around the airplanes. Huge, intensely bright lights illuminated the airplane that towered above me.

I bounded up the metal steps towards the aircraft. I was eager to get out of the cold wind, and even more eager to board 'my' airplane.

Once I reached the landing at the top of the ramp I felt as though I had truly *arrived.* It was one of those moments of complete and utter satisfaction in my life. I wanted to savor it. If I were wearing a hat, I would have tossed it high into the air.

After years of dead-end jobs, overnight jobs, and low-paying jobs, I had actually pulled myself up from that situation by planning and reaching a goal, – the goal of working for Federal Express. My standing here at this big beautiful jet made that dream so real, more real even, than when I got my ID Badge.

My entire being was awash with the pride of achievement. If I felt this good, Fred Smith, who created Federal Express out of thin air, must feel like a magician when he looks at these jets.

I do believe in magic, but not the kind that makes something appear due to the waving of a wand. I believe in the kind of magic that makes things appear because of the workings of a man's (or woman's) brain.

I turned my eyes to feast on the sight of the massive jet.

It looked like it was a city block in length. The deep-purple-over-white paint job on the jet was attention-grabbing for sure. The name "Federal" was painted in huge square white letters which contrasted sharply against the deep purple fuselage. Just below the word 'Federal', the word 'Express' was painted in bold orange letters against the white part of the jet.

My eyes continued to sweep like scrubbing

bubbles along the length of the purple and white fuselage all the way to the rear of the plane. There, the T-shaped tail towered into the air above the body of the plane like the torch over the Statue of Liberty. I had heard the 727 referred to as a T-Bird, and I guessed this T-shaped tail was the reason.

As I stood outside the door of the T-Bird I brushed my wind-blown hair out of my eyes to see the freight being loaded into the airplane. The freight was in metal containers that I had learned from the Jump Seat manual were called modules.

The modules were lifted up to the jet's open cargo door on a platform that elevated from the back of a truck. Once a module was at the cargo door, ramp workers in dark blue uniforms pushed it into the aircraft, and then rolled it toward the back of the plane. Once in the correct spot, the ramp agents secured the module to the floor. There was very little wasted space surrounding the modules in the jet's cargo hold.

The plane jostled a bit as each module was loaded. As I watched more and more cargo being loaded onto the plane, I became aware - keenly aware, of the ever-increasing weight of the airplane. I began to have serious doubts about the plane actually being *able* to fly.

Although I had flown all of my life and knew logically that planes could fly, all of that went out the window at this point. This plane seemed *too* heavy to fly.

Just when I had become convinced that it was simply impossible for the plane to get off the ground, another Federal Express 727 streaked across the full October moon, briefly silhouetted there like a witch on her broom.

"Wow! " I said aloud.

My confidence had been restored and I stepped aboard the jet. To my right was a huge nylon web behind which were the modules. In front of me was a door to a restroom and to my left was the open cockpit door. I turned left and stepped through this door, into the cockpit.

It was the very first time I had ever been inside the cockpit of a jet.

The cockpit smelled like a combination of

sunbaked leather and the faint smell of the machine oil that my grandfather used to clean his hunting rifle. There were two battleship-gray jump seats lined up on the left of the cockpit, directly behind the Captain's seat.

The Flight Engineer was at his console on the right side of the cockpit.

"Welcome aboard," he said, "My name is Wes. You must be Brenda Copeland. "

"Yes, I am," I replied as I showed him my Federal Express photo ID which was clipped to my jacket.

He looked at it and said, "You're good to go, take either one of those seats."

I sat down in the seat just inside the cockpit door and pulled my carry-on into the space between me the jump seat in front of me.

"Have you ever jump seated before? " Wes asked.

"No," I replied. 'But how hard could it be?' I thought.

"OK, I'll give you the rundown."

He picked up a brown paper grocery bag on the floor next to his console and began turning down its edges as he spoke:

"The second most important rule in the cockpit is to never grab the Captain's oxygen mask." He pointed to a mask just to the left and slightly behind the Captain's seat and said, "That's the Captain's oxygen mask."

He then pointed to an oxygen mask to my left on the wall and said, "That's your oxygen mask." While explaining, he continued turning down the edges of the bag.

"What's the first most important rule in the cockpit?" I asked, figuratively pricking up my ears in order to hear this most important rule.

He answered in a serious tone, "Never, *ever* ride jump seat without bringing cookies."

I laughed. I had already been advised by my coworkers to bring cookies, and thank goodness I listened. Sticking out of my carry-on bag was a box of chocolate chip, windmill, and sugar cookies which I had carefully baked . . . OK, OK, I bought them at Kroger.

"Roger that." I replied, trying to sound crew-like. "I've got three kinds of cookies with me."

"Great." the Flight Engineer replied with a smile. He then nodded his head at a headset on the wall to my left.

"You can wear that headset if you want to listen to the communications between the air traffic control and the pilots."

Then he placed the bag on which he had been working onto the floor next to my seat. He didn't have to tell me what it was for. I know a flight sickness bag when I see one. (Just ask my sister, Pam.)

Wes was just wrapping up his instructions when the Captain and First Officer entered the cockpit like 'The Men in Black'. Only they wore navy. They took their jackets off and hung them in an area just inside the cockpit door and to the right of the Flight Engineer's console.

The Captain looked at me, lifted his pilot's hat and smoothed his thick hair back as he said, "I see we only have one jump seater tonight. I'm Captain Sawyer and this is First Officer Stevens."

First Officer Stevens nodded at me.

"Nice to meet you, I'm Brenda Copeland."

Once introductions were exchanged, the pilots climbed into their respective seats. The

Captain sat in the left seat and the First Officer sat in the right seat.

I had already sat in the Captain's seat. Prior to the pilots' arrival, I had asked the Flight Engineer to snap a picture of me in the Captain's seat, to mark what I considered to be a momentous event in my life. He kindly snapped the photo. (See cover . . .)

Since it looked like things were about to get underway, I buckled my five-way seat belt four ways, one strap over each shoulder and one strap around each side of my hips, the way the Flight Engineer had shown me. All belts could be released simultaneously with a quick turn of a release knob in the center.

A ramp agent entered the cockpit and briefly

discussed a Weight and Balance sheet with the First Officer.

Then he said "Have a safe flight." and he left, shutting the cabin door behind him.

There was something so final in the shutting of the cockpit door. We were committed now.

I felt like an official part of the crew once I strapped into my seat and was wearing my own headset. I put it on at a slight angle so I could still hear any requests from the flight crew. I could hear pilots talking to air traffic control. Mixed with a slight crackle of static their communications sounded robot-like.

'Man, this is really happening.' I thought.

'Of course it's happening' I chided myself.

But things felt a little surreal. There is something about doing things in the middle of the night, when you are normally asleep that alters reality ever so slightly. Especially when that reality is so dramatically different than anything you've ever done before. It's almost like you are dreaming. Or you are swimming under the ocean, where everything is shut out except that fish or coral or sea fan right in front of you.

Pilots and other Federal Express employees who work the overnight shift are given tips on dealing with the disruption of the natural sleep cycle or 'Circadian Rhythm.' Circadian Rhythm refers to the natural biological cycle of sleeping and waking which repeats itself within approximately every 24-hours. 'Circa' means near and 'Dia' means day, thus the word Circadian Rhythm. One of the effects of sleep deprivation is a craving for sweets. No wonder they wanted jump seaters to bring cookies.

The Captain ran his hands over the instruments on a panel above and to the right of his head and asked, "Where're the lights?"

"He's *got* to be kidding." I thought.

The aircraft hummed to life and was pushed back from its loading area. Then the massive jet, with its outspread wings full of fuel and its belly full of tons of freight, rolled heavily towards a runway. It paused in front of a runway where other purple-and-white Federal Express jets were taking off one after another in an awesome display of power, speed, and fierce can-do attitude.

Jets that had lifted up into the night sky in the distance fanned out towards their various destinations in an array of lights like blurry stars. The sight reminded me a little of Van Gogh's painting 'Starry Night.'

A massive DC-10 took off just before our jet. As it hurtled down the runway, the First Officer simply said, "Heavy Metal." I love understatement, don't you?

Then our plane turned onto the runway and jostled to a halt.

The Captain asked, "Brenda, are you ready to fly?"

"Do I have a choice?" I answered from the back.

The Captain laughed.

Not to say I was chickening out. I wasn't.

I really think that I have 'airplane' in my DNA.

I love the *style* of airplanes from the patterns on the seats to the uniforms of the flight attendants and pilots.

I love airplane food and the perfectly-sized dinnerware with its airline logo on everything including the napkins.

I love the view from an airplane of clouds or

of the ocean, or even of moody gray streaks of rain.

I love the view of a sprawling city at night. It looks like a jeweler's case of precious jewels glittering against black velvet.

And, I *especially* love the moment an airplane lifts off the ground. At the moment the wheels lift off of the ground, the airplane becomes something greatly superior to what it was while earthbound. The moment of takeoff is like the moment a piece of coal becomes a diamond.

No, I was not chickening out.

However, while I normally enjoy the view of takeoff from my usual window seat on commercial flights, the view from the cockpit is different. It is scary - really scary. I was used to feeling cosseted by the enclosed interior of a commercial airplane cabin. The wall in front of me on commercial airplanes gave me a sensation of having a protective layer between me and the ground.

In contrast, in the cockpit I felt vulnerable and exposed. There was no wall, just the front windows through which I could clearly see the long, lighted concrete runway and the many black skid marks that patterned it.

Suddenly the engines roared with power like a giant stallion announcing to a challenger that he's ready for the fight. My palms started to sweat. It occurred to me that I must have been crazy to think that I liked being in the 'thick of things.'

The airplane surged forward. I felt pushed back in my seat. Faster and faster the powerful jet surged, mimicking the surge of adrenaline in my body. I felt as though I were on the point of an arrow that was screaming towards its target.

'Hold it! I'm not ready for this! 'I yelled in my mind. My heart pounded. The plane was now hurtling down the runway. I always say a prayer before any takeoff, and I said a particularly intense one for this takeoff. Then I covered my face with my hands. I just couldn't watch. Puck, puck, puuucck! "

It took about 30 seconds for the plane to lift off into the wild black yonder. I know because I was counting down the last seconds of my life.

While I was dealing with my yellow streak, the pilots were dealing with the takeoff. They were extremely focused during the takeoff. I had learned from studying the Jump Seat manual that jump seaters are not to distract the pilots.

We are not to speak until the plane is over 10,000 feet in the air. I was fine with that - far be it for me to want to distract the very people who have my life in their hands. From my seat, I could see the altimeter clicking ever increasing numbers until it passed the 10,000 foot mark.

After the plane reached the 10,000 foot mark and above, the mood in the cockpit relaxed noticeably.

"Can I get anyone something to drink?" the Flight Engineer asked.

"Thanks. Coffee – black." the Captain answered.

"Nothing for me." the First Officer said.

Then the Flight Engineer looked at me, wanting my answer.

"Water would be fine with me. " I said.

Wes left the cockpit and in a couple of minutes returned with a frosty bottle of Crystal Geyser water for me and coffee for the Captain. He carefully handed these to us in the dimly lit cockpit. The cockpit is dark except for the glowing instrument lights scattered around and the ambient light from the night sky. This, along with the tight quarters, makes for a cozy and seductive atmosphere.

The Captain asked, "Did that gorgeous woman bring cookies?" (I told you it was dark.)

I passed the box of cookies up to the front where the Captain took a couple of the cookies and passed the box of them around to the other men. He took a bite of cookie, washing it down with the black coffee.

The jet with its three and one-half crewmembers and tons of golden packages cruised smoothly in the moonlit sky towards Atlanta. At one point during the flight, the Captain turned the controls over to the First Officer telling him, "Just keep the purple side up."

"Hmmm," I thought, "If that is all there is to it, I could probably fly the thing."

About half-way to Atlanta, the jet flew into some storm clouds. Again, the tension in the cockpit became heightened. The turbulence wasn't too bad, but there were electrical charges in the night sky. Electrical snakes started crawling on the nose and windows of the jet. They picked up the purple color of the jet, and a purple glow gilded everything in the cabin.

"That's St. Elmo's Fire." the Flight Engineer informed me, as his faced glowed with purple.

It was surreal.

By the time the jet started its descent into Atlanta, I was determined to watch every single minute of the landing. I had realized during the flight that if something happened it may be my last chance of seeing anything, and I wanted to see it, even if it was just a weed growing up through a crack in the tarmac.

As the airplane descended, I held onto my handbag because I thought the landing would be a little rough. I must have had a lot of seats back near the engines on commercial flights because the sensation of landing from the cockpit was surprisingly quiet and gentle in comparison. The cockpit seemed round, and I had no sense of the elongated aircraft body. I felt as though I were in a round bubble that gently descended from the sky onto the runway.

Glenda the Good Witch in the Wizard of Oz probably had the same sensation when she was gently deposited in Oz in a huge bubble.

Good job guys!

Chapter 2

FRED SMITH

"A man's grasp should exceed his reach."

Robert Browning

Robert Browning could have been referring to Frederick W. Smith in his sentiment; "A man's grasp should exceed his reach." Fred Smith, also known as 'FWS' is the founder of Federal Express, and a legend in his own time for creating such a wildly successful and iconic company.

While I worked for Federal Express, Fred Smith was also the CEO. Although Fred Smith was fit, he was prematurely gray. Maybe that was due to heredity or maybe it was due to the stress he underwent while bringing his dream of Federal Express into reality.

His Herculean efforts to bring Federal Express to fruition are well known by most employees. He originally presented the idea for the company in a class assignment while attending Yale. The paper received only a mediocre grade. I don't know the name of the professor who graded the paper, but I sure know the name Frederick W. Smith.

Fred Smith gave a weekly address to the employees on the company's closed circuit television. Speaking for myself and I'm sure, lots of other employees, it was always inspiring to hear Mr. Smith rally the troops so to speak. No matter how successful Federal Express appears to be, it was reassuring to hear from our fearless leader. He would remind us that he didn't pay us, the customer did. Or he and one of the top brass would encourage us to enjoy life, or remind us that there was always competition out there. We also were informed of various new services or new ideas that were to be implemented by the company.

Besides keeping his employees informed and inspired, FWS served another purpose - that of fashion icon. His television address would be on Thursday, and by the following Monday, many middle management males would be wearing a tie identical to what FWS had worn on TV the previous week.

I'm sure the salespeople in the menswear departments around Memphis wondered why a certain tie would be so in demand each week.

(Well now you know.)

Chapter 3

FRED'S MONEY

One thing most of the employees of Federal Express know, is that you do not fool with the corporate assets aka, 'Fred's Money.' The company takes Fred's Money very seriously and expects the employees to take *care* of the money, not *take* the money. There is sophisticated surveillance in vulnerable areas of the company as well as checks and balances to protect the assets and money. An employee will almost certainly get caught if they take money or property from the eagle-eyed Company.

There is, however, the odd duck who thinks he will not get caught. I know of one instance of a pilot playing fast and loose with company money. Pilots from all over the world send resumes in the hope of being hired by FedEx, and most of them would certainly be grateful or smart or honest enough not to fool with Fred's Money. But this particular pilot must have not gotten the memo.

The pilot bought several lunches while he was on a layover between flights in a West Coast city. Upon his return to Memphis, he turned in his expense report with receipts attached. He must not have realized that expense accounts are audited.

His manager, of course, caught the

discrepancy. The manager called the hotel where the bill originated and verified that room service in the amount of eighty dollars was signed by the pilot in question.

The pilot was called in to his manager's office and was asked to explain the very high lunch bill. He admitted that he got carried away and charged over eighty dollars for lunch for some family members and that he would be glad to pay it back immediately.

His offer wasn't accepted.

But his resignation was.

Chapter 4

PEOPLE-SERVICE-PROFIT

FedEx has a motto of People Service Profit, or PSP for short. The simple message is that if you take care of the People, in turn they will provide the best Service possible and logically, Profits will result. Most employees understand this concept, but occasionally someone drops the ball.

One occasion that I recall of someone dropping the ball, was when a senior manager was showing Fred Smith the training department where I worked as a secretary. The manager, I'll call 'R' showed Mr. Smith the classrooms, and introduced him to each training specialist as well as to the students. I was eager to meet Fred Smith, who I knew would pass my cubicle.

The manager walked FWS right past my cubicle and around the corner. I knew FWS had been introduced to every single person in my department, except for me. I immediately felt slighted and let down. Before 'R' and FWS had walked half-way past my cubicle, Fred Smith turned around, leaving 'R' standing there and came back to my cubicle and stepped inside. He leaned over slightly and introduced himself as he shook my hand and gave me a conspiratorial wink and a smile.

My spirits soared. I knew that he 'gets it.' Hard not to like a guy like that! And even

harder not to do the best job possible for a man who treats you as a valuable person, as valuable as any other person who works for him.

That's not the first time I had met Fred Smith. A couple of years earlier, I was sent to the office of second-in-command Ted Weise's office to work for him while his Administrative Assistant was recovering from surgery. FWS' office was around the corner and one day he came over and seemed a little surprised that the regular secretary wasn't there, but instead, there I sat, (probably with a silly grin on my face.) He introduced himself. My impression was that he's a man with a sense of fun, who wants people to feel at ease in his presence.

I may have had a silly grin, but at least I didn't become unhinged in his presence. There

are several stories about people who become unglued around FWS, such as the lady who talked to him after a meeting, then left the conference room. But not before she walked into a storage closet first.

Fortunately, I only come unglued when on jump seat. (And it helped that there were no storage closets in my area.)

Chapter 5

MISTAKEN IDENTITY

Linda and I got a small taste of what FWS may put up with one time when we jump seated to the Newark, NJ airport to visit a friend.

Our friend, G, likes to spoil us. Over the years, we have enjoyed wonderful trips with her, whether it is to the Bahamas, or England, or Miami. On this particular visit, we jump-seated into Newark, which was the nearest airport to where G lives.

After landing at Newark airport, the FedEx 727 nosed up to a chain-link fence in the FedEx ramp area. Once it stopped and was secured, the Ramp Agent came aboard.

Normally the Agent greets the Captain and the Crew first. Instead, he seemed very nervous as he looked at Linda, whose last name is Smith. He stammered, "M' M' Ms Smith, your, your, ca, car is here." He immediately took Linda's' bag and offered to take mine. We knew that crewmembers are not to carry jump seater's luggage, so we wondered what was going on with this Ramp Agent.

We looked through the cockpit windows and saw a silver limousine parked just on the opposite side of the fence. Seeing a limo at an airport is a common thing these days, but back

then, they were very rare. People took taxies or shuttle vans to get to their destinations.

We had been told to look for a green Taurus. Instead here was this luxurious limousine before us. Its immaculately-dressed driver, Bob, was entering the ramp area through a gate in the fence.

We now realized that the Ramp Agent must have thought that Linda was a relative of Fred Smith!

We left it at that.

At the bottom of the ramp, Bob took the luggage and we followed him to the car.

Linda said, "Bob, we thought you were going to pick us up outside the AA terminal."

Bob responded, "My instructions were to park *under* the wing!"

We all laughed at that, knowing that G wanted to show that we were important to her, even if we were just friends, and no one famous.

Chapter 6

PURPLE BLOOD

FedEx *is* its employees, like tiny fish that gather together to make something bigger and more intimidating than themselves as individuals so as to ward off predators. It's no wonder that FedEx has been so successful. The winning spirit started at the top, and spread throughout the rank and file employees from there.

Employees at Federal Express often describe themselves as having "purple blood," the purple color coming from the purple part of the purple and orange Federal Express colors. They are rightfully proud to be part of FedEx.

I was no exception.

I too, was proud to work for Federal Express. I surrounded myself with all things Federal Express. I had a huge print of a Federal Express jet flying on a moonlit night on the wall over my credenza. I had a model of a Federal Express jet on my desk, on which I wrote my name on the front as I had seen names on Federal Express jets. I drank from a Federal Express coffee cup. And I used a pen from a walnut pen holder on which was mounted a pewter replica of a Federal Express 727 jet.

Yes, I was proud to work for Federal Express, or FedEx as it is now known.

The name change came within a few years after my coming on board, when the name 'Federal Express' was replaced with 'FedEx.'

FedEx with a capital F, capital E. The purple and white jets were repainted white, with a purple tail and the name Federal Express was replaced with 'FedEx.' The name Federal Express was also changed to FedEx on all of the Company's stationery, vans, signage, signature blocks, apparel, coffee mugs, t-shirts, pens - basically on any item where one would expect a Federal Express logo.

Chapter 7

NEITHER RAIN NOR SLEET . . .
WELL, MAYBE SLEET . . .

One wintry day, at about lunch time, I heard a tapping sound on the window near my desk. When I looked up, I saw that sleet was beginning to fall from the grey clouds outside. I was concerned because I had a 35-mile trip home and I could see that the sleet was rapidly sticking to the cold glass of the window.

My boss walked through the area and announced, "You should all leave as soon as possible, looks like we have a weather day."

Federal Express pays its employees if the weather forces them to go home and that day is recorded as an inclement weather day.

Although my boss told everyone to go home, it was clear to me that I may have to spend the night at the office. Fortunately FedEx is prepared for most events, especially weather-related events. There are showers in the lady's lounge as well as a sofa in an alcove of the lounge. I kept a kit of toiletries in my car for just such an event so I was prepared to make it an all-nighter.

Luckily, one of my coworkers I'll call 'W' saved me from that fate when she invited me to stay with her as her house was near the office. I gladly accepted her kind invitation. W and I carefully made our way to her car which had ice all over it.

She had to scrape ice off of the windshield with her ID badge before we got into it. As she drove out of the parking lot, we could see numerous other FedEx employees driving out of the parking lot as well.

Although W's car had great traction, by the time we were only a couple of miles away from the office we were in trouble. The roads were so slick that many cars and even tractor-trailers were abandoned. W and I knew that we weren't going anywhere. We looked around to find a place to spend the night.

We could see a motel across the street with a large number of cars surrounding it like cows around a watering hole. We abandoned W's car and carefully made our way across the slippery street to the motel.

The lobby was packed with people and we recognized many FedEx employees. Neither W nor I had a credit card or enough cash for our room. However, to our relief, another FedEx employee put our room on his credit card, which we promised to repay. We went to our room to check it out. The room seemed clean and had two double beds which were nice.

After W and I checked out the room, we headed to the motel's restaurant as we were both hungry.

The restaurant, like the lobby, was packed with people. Amazingly there was an empty booth with red vinyl seats across the room.

W and I quickly pounced on this as our animal instincts for survival were quickly taking over our usual civilized manners.

A waitress came over without a menu and said in matter-of-act tone, "What d'ya want, toast and eggs?"

"Do you have any hamburgers? " I asked.

"Nope we're out of everything except eggs, toast, coffee and tea.   W and I mulled over our options.

Then W ordered eggs and toast and I ordered toast and eggs.

The next morning, the streets were clear enough that we were able to retrieve the car and go to work, wearing the same clothes that we had worn the day before.

Chapter 8

COME FLY WITH ME

Federal Express started out in business with a fleet of small Falcon jets. The company purchased some of these jets from Pan American World Airline in a deal which was transacted in Freeport, Bahamas. At that time my father was the Director of Air Traffic Control at Freeport International Airport. He met some of the company's pilots when they came into the business office to pay landing fees, and he invited them to come up to the tower.

While in the tower, these pilots recommended to my father that he buy some stock in a new company called Federal Express when it went public. My father didn't heed their advice, a decision he (and I) regret to this day.

Naturally, as package volumes continued to increase, all of the Falcons except for a couple were phased out as the company bought larger planes, such as 727s, DC-10s and MD-11s. I know that one remaining Falcon is displayed in the Smithsonian Institution and another is displayed in the Flight Training Center of FedEx.

FedEx's Flight Training Center is state-of-the-art, and as such, has the latest equipment for training their large number of pilots. Any new pilot or new plane in the fleet brought the need for remedial flight training. I was working in the Flight Training Department when FedEx purchased an MD-11. FedEx jets usually have a name painted on them, near the front end, left side of the jet and painted on that area of this new MD-11 was the name 'Phoenix'.

The MD-11 was the latest jet out, with modern features and one big advantage over other jets of the time. The big advantage the MD-11 had is that it requires only a two-person crew rather than the standard three-person crew used in other commercial jets. Using two crew members rather than three is a money saver. The MD-11 also has what is called a "glass cockpit. " Previous to the MD-11, jets had gauges on their dashboards, sort of like a British roadster. But the MD-11 has a modern looking glass dash with information displayed by LED-like lights.

Soon an MD-11 simulator was installed in Flight Training.

One day I was invited to ride in the MD-11 simulator. Of course I said yes. I can be really brave in a simulator.

The simulator cockpit was huge and looked almost like an actual cockpit. The only difference I saw was that the simulator had an area in the back where an instructor sat next to a control panel with a selection of buttons that corresponded with different situations that a pilot may encounter. The bag of tricks ranged from a rabbit running in front of the jet to a vehicle on the runway, to tire blowouts, and many others. The windshield of the cockpit displayed a virtual view of a runway, and also displayed any of the emergencies that the instructor chose. I strapped into a jump seat just as I would in an actual airplane.

Then the MD-11 took off.

I was *amazed* to feel the G-force as though the aircraft truly had picked up speed and lifted off the runway. Once 'airborne,' we buzzed the Clark Tower in Memphis and flew under the Mississippi River Bridge. I could see the rivets of the bridge through the windshield. I was sure the tail would hit, but it didn't. We flew to Hong Kong airport which was surrounded by hills. We ran over a rabbit. Then we headed back to Memphis.

You know you are in the Memphis airspace

because the name "ELVIS" appears in hot pink lights on the glass dash. That is simply one of the coolest things I've ever seen!

Chapter 9

CHRISTMAS

Christmas at FedEx is one of the many times that FedEx uses to benefit the Memphis community. FedEx employees can volunteer to pack food baskets to hand out to the needy in Memphis.

One Christmas season I volunteered to help pack food baskets. I worked along with dozens of other employees in the hub. We worked like Santa's helpers at a conveyor belt, adding canned goods and other foods to boxes that, once filled, were loaded onto trucks for distribution to the needy in Memphis. The temperature in the hub was very cold, and my hands felt frozen. Nevertheless, I, as well as the other employees, kept smiling and joking in the spirit of helping out others.

Oftentimes at Christmas there would be contests to see who could decorate their office or cubicle the best. The Call Center was decorated to the hilt. Service Centers had Christmas trees in their lobbies. Employees might have little trees, Santa figurines, angels, nativity sets, or candy canes on their desks.

Occasionally children from local grade schools would walk through the hallways singing Christmas carols. It wasn't unusual to see a Santa or two walking around dropping off candy canes and wishing each employee a

Merry Christmas.

There were Christmas parties too. One year I was placed in charge of planning one for my division. The Friday night of the party, everything from the decorations, to the food, to the music and door prizes were what I had hoped they would be. My husband and I enjoyed the festivities and we stayed until everyone had gone home.

My sister Linda's FedEx Christmas party was to be the next night, Saturday, in Montana. As a service agent in a Business Service Center she was on the front lines handling the Christmas rush. Linda loves Christmas and would be in an upbeat mood even after an 11- hour day taking an avalanche of packages from customers hoping to get their gifts delivered on time to family, or friends. The only thing she complained about was that she had nothing to wear to her Christmas party.

After my party had ended, I changed into casual clothes, boxed up my dress, shoes, and even the necklace I wore and FedEx'ed them to Linda. I sent them before midnight, which was the cutoff time to send a package from the airport BSC.

The service agent who took my package must have thought it strange of me to leave the service center barefoot. I had to because, although I had brought a change of clothes, I had forgotten a change of shoes. Somehow, without my shoes, and the lateness of the hour, I felt a little like Cinderella, leaving the ball and having my gown turn into rags. It was worth it though as Linda was delighted to receive a complete ensemble to wear to her Christmas party. That was her Christmas gift from me.

Speaking of Christmas gifts, I generally received a Christmas card from the various bosses for whom I worked over my eleven years at FedEx. That is until I went to work at Flight Training. Another Administrative Assistant, I'll call 'H', and I supported a group of five Flight Training Managers, all of whom were pilots. At Christmas time. H and I each got so many fruit baskets, poinsettias, and boxes of chocolates from these bosses that we had to make a couple of trips to our cars to carry them all.

Those pilots certainly debunked the myth that pilots are cheap.

A common joke between pilots in the Flight Training Department is, "What's a penny between pilots?"

"Copper wire."

Chapter 10

CATCH ME IF YOU CAN

I am the daughter of a mother who worked for Eastern Airlines, and a father who was the Director of Air Traffic Control at Freeport International Airport in the Bahamas. As such if there is one thing I respect and admire it is the aviation profession. I have never missed a flight in my life. I have been bumped before, and I have had to change airplanes due to equipment problems. But I have never missed a flight due to my running late to the airport.

To my horror, my unblemished record was in danger of being broken and broken in a most public way. That is because my entire division was to attend *the* business meeting of the year in Atlanta and they were all aboard the American Airlines flight that I was about to miss.

They all would *know* what a terrible, disorganized, unprofessional, and undependable employee I was. (Have I left anything out?)

I was at risk of missing this flight because on my way to the airport, I ran into several unexpected obstacles. The first obstacle presented itself as a torrential downpour. My car's windshield wipers simply couldn't keep up with the deluge, and I had to slow down. Since I had a 35-mile trip to the airport, even a little bit of a delay per mile really added up. My stress was building as I watched the digital clock in my Ford Thunderbird chalk up minutes faster than I had ever seen.

About two miles from the airport, just when I was sure I would make it to the airport on time, I was stopped by the second obstacle - railroad gates coming down in front of my car! I felt my blood pressure go up, although I had never had a blood pressure problem before. Due to the rain, I'm sure no one heard the expletive that was not deleted. The train was a long one and by the time the gates finally lifted, my nerves were stretched, well, like that copper wire between pilots.

I made it to the airport, but in my panic, I created the third obstacle that delayed me - I parked my car at the opposite end of the airport from my airline! In my right mind, I would have parked nearest the airline terminal for American Airlines. I was out of my car and walking in underground parking when I realized my mistake.

I asked a man who was driving past me in a red truck if he would mind giving me a ride to the American Airlines terminal. I would normally never take a ride with a stranger, but, hey my job comes first!

The man dropped me off alive at my terminal. I thanked him and dashed inside with my carry-on bag, a grey and pink Pegasus. In all modesty, I thought it went well with my pink silk suit, with teal silk blouse and bird of paradise pin.

But, I was all dressed up, with maybe no place to go, unless I really hurried. My pink designer heels were clicking along what seemed like miles of floors. I kept on running even after I was on the rolling sidewalk. To my relief, I saw another employee, a Bigwig, running just behind me, obviously late herself. I guess misery does love company.

I said to her, "Thank goodness I've been doing aerobics!"

She laughed as much as she could as she too was pretty winded.

We both made it onto the flight at the very last second. My face was beet red from exertion and panic. As I walked down the aisle, Big Wigs and Little Wigs alike fixed their eyes on me like

Monarch butterflies landing on a tropical tree. I took my assigned seat directly across the aisle from my boss and a coworker who were looking at me with quizzical looks.

I turned to them as I was fastening my seatbelt and said;

"Glad y'all made it."

Chapter 11

A GIRL'S BEST FRIEND . . .

FedEx often has meetings where various employees are honored for their outstanding work. I attended many of these types of meetings, but one stands out in my memory. Instead of being held on-site in a meeting room, it was held in a grand ballroom of a nearby luxury hotel.

Richly patterned carpeting and sparkling chandeliers greeted my friend I'll call 'D' and me as we entered the ballroom. The ballroom was set up with hundreds of chairs, as well as a stage. We could see the awards which set on a large table on the stage. The awards were tall black trophies with a cut glass diamond the size of a small apple on top. They were called Diamond Awards.

Because the awards were so heavy and cumbersome, the hosting manager said he would call the name of each person who was to receive an Award. He said that we would adjourn for lunch after the names were called. Since the meeting was over at lunchtime, people could pick up their award after lunch and carry it back to their offices.

I sat with my friend D and we applauded as each name was read. Then the meeting was adjourned and we headed out for lunch.

Instead of turning left down the aisle with me, D turned right in the direction of the stage. She quickly walked up to the host and said something to him. I was impatient, because I wanted to eat. (You know me.) Anyway, the manager called me up to the stage. Now I was really perplexed. He picked up one of the Diamond Awards and handed it to me. I looked at it and saw my name engraved on it. I found it hard to believe my name was on such a nice award.

Apparently my name had been omitted from the list that the host used to identify recipients of the award. However, D had seen an award with my name on it when she first walked into the room. (Does she have an eagle eye or what?) She had enough grace to keep her discovery quiet, so I didn't suspect a thing.

When my name had not been called, she made sure to tell the manager. (Thank you D!) I received the Diamond Award to no applause as the room was empty by then.

Don't worry about me, I displayed my Diamond Award prominently in my cubicle and made *sure* to rub it into people's faces for years to come.

The person who recommended me for the Diamond Award, was my first manager at FedEx, 'J.' J was a truly wonderful boss, who was never mean or petty with any of his employees. He was a pleasant, well-groomed, and neatly dressed man with brown hair and eyes. J couldn't tolerate clutter and his desk was always clear, except when he just had to put something on it like paperwork for a

Performance Review. I learned to work at my desk without putting a lot unnecessary paperwork on it while working. I'm glad to have worked for such a nice boss my first few years with FedEx.

J wasn't the only nice person at FedEx, there were lots of them. I met one of these nice people one day when I stepped into an elevator to ride up to the third floor where I worked. A blond woman was already on the elevator. She was dressed in a flowery dress and was wearing a necklace made of a silvery gray abalone shell with silver on the edges. I complimented the necklace to her.

A few months later, that same woman came by my work area and surprised me by presenting me with the necklace. I tried not to take it, but she was generous and insisted that I take it, which I did. (What could I do, daddy didn't buy the FedEx stock, LOL.)

Another generous person at FedEx was a manager, 'C', who arrived in Memphis from Britain in order to tour our Business Service Centers. He had arrived a day late due to a family emergency, and my manager, who was to show him around was unavoidably detained. I knew the British manager's itinerary (since I was the one who created it), so I drove him in my black Thunderbird to various offices of FedEx. I left him in the capable hands of a Business Service Center Manager and returned to my department.

A couple of weeks after C's visit, I received a package with a return address in Great Britain. Inside was a Thank You note from C as well as a lovely blue and white Wedgwood Jasperware plate. It was really good of him to do that, although I was just doing my job.

Chapter 12

DOUBLE TROUBLE in the
BUBBLE and Other Trips

My sister Linda and I are twins and mom sometimes refers to us as "Double Trouble. " For our double birthday in June we always try to fly somewhere interesting. One year we decided to celebrate in Germany and Switzerland. On that trip Linda generously paid for my ticket on Swissair as my Birthday gift from her. (She could afford to pay since the interline discount between FedEx and Swissair was 90 %.)

Once aboard the Swissair 747, we were seated in the bubble area of the massive jet. There we were, Double Trouble in the Bubble. Mom would have gotten a kick out of that scenario. Our flight took off at about 9:00 at night from JFK International, and in about six hours, the light from the rising sun revealed the Swiss Alps below. They looked just like a giant chocolate sundae with the chocolate running down the sides of peaks of vanilla ice cream.

I must have had chocolate on the mind because I saw chocolate in everything. The Swissair jet had a dark chocolate above a milk chocolate colored stripe around the body of the plane. The pillows and blankets were also chocolate colored and the Flight Attendants freely handed out Swiss chocolates.

My coworkers back in Memphis were happy to see that I had chocolate on the brain, because I brought them a huge, shiny gold box of Swiss chocolates. The box had a picture of pink roses on the lid. I placed it on a desk in the middle of the room and opened it for anyone to help themselves to all that chocolate decadence.

Switzerland was a wonderful destination to celebrate our birthday but one of my favorite destinations for another birthday was here in America - Yellowstone National Park.

At the time we took that trip, Linda was living in Billings, Montana. I jump seated into Great Falls, Montana, and she picked me up in her frost-covered Thunderbird. It was still dark. I was tired as I had worked a full day the day before, then stayed up for hours to catch my jump seat, then another couple of hours on the flight. I climbed into the roomy back seat of her car and quickly fell asleep while she drove southeast towards Billings.

Morning dawned as I slept, and Linda asked, "Brenda, are you awake?" I was in a netherworld, not quite sound asleep, but not quite awake. I heard her and opened my eyes - well, maybe one eye . . .

"Yeah, I'm awake." I slurred.

"You just have to see this!"

I sat up and looked out the side window. I saw a golden panorama of cut hayfields that stretched to the horizon. Dagger-sharp rays of the morning sun caught the frost at just the right angle to make it sparkle like crushed diamonds spread across the fields.

I saw a massive stack of square bales of hay in one of these fields. It was easily as big as a three-story building. Each bale of hay looked like a giant gold ingot in the glittering frost. Deer, that looked tiny in comparison to the Fort Knox of hay, ate their fill along the bottom edges.

We drove past the exit to Billings and on to Red Lodge, a small town that is the gateway to the Beartooth Pass. The Beartooth Pass leads into Wyoming and the Northeast entrance to Yellowstone. Red Lodge is practically stuck in the cowboy days. If I were to assign a sound that would evoke the feeling of Red Lodge, it would be the sound of rowels spinning on spurs.

We saw a restaurant with a 'Home-Cooking' sign and parked the car and went inside.

It felt good to get out of the cold and into the restaurant full of people. And, I must say that my hearty breakfast of eggs, bacon, and iced tea tasted particularly good after a night of jump seating.

When Linda and I left the restaurant, we headed to a shop next to the restaurant. We walked past vehicles, mainly pickup trucks, parked along the street in front of the shop. I was shocked to see the many wild animals and/or animal heads that were in the truck beds.

This clearly was a major hunting area.

When I mentioned seeing all of the animal heads to Linda, she replied;

"You haven't seen anything. Three years ago when my ex (a musician) came here, he garnered resentment because of his popularity with the women here. One night, when he left his singing gig at a popular nightspot, he walked out to the car, only to find a deer inside of it. It was propped up in the driver's seat with its hoofs over the steering wheel."

I had heard many stories of the drama between Linda and her ex, who, although an exceptionally talented musician, failed miserably when it came to staying sober, or staying faithful. Even so, I couldn't believe she had never told me that story before.

"You didn't put that deer in the car did you?" I joked.

"Well, I certainly had reason to, but, that night I had lent him my car, and there's no way I would have done that to my car.

"Oh, no, not your car!"

"Well, the good thing about it is - he checked into rehab and never drank again after that."

We were laughing as we entered the shop, which was filled with stuffed animals in different vignettes that they may have experienced in life. Besides displaying wildlife, the store basically sold souvenirs, camping supplies, t-shirts, bison jerky, and the like. I saw a t-shirt with a picture of a grizzled prospector standing next to his pack mule, with the words, "I got my ass across the Pass." I laughed at that. I knew he was referring to the Beartooth Pass, which was the next leg of our trip. The Pass starts out in a valley near Red Lodge with mountains on either side and ends in Wyoming.

We left the store, hopped into the car, and headed for the Pass. It was about a seventy-mile drive across the Pass into Wyoming. We drove higher and higher up narrow roads that switched back on themselves several times on the edge of the mountain.

I looked out of the passenger side window to see no road edge between the car and the valley below us. As we drove higher up the mountain, the pretty creek in the valley looked like a piece of ribbon and the deer and antelope looked like miniature figurines if you could make them out at all. As we neared the top of the Pass, we saw long poles along the road so as to mark the road's edge, for the snowplow.

At the top of the Pass we saw a massive rock formation. It was triangular in shape, coming to a sharp point which cut into the Montana sky.

"That's the 'bear tooth' and the reason this area is called the Beartooth Pass." Linda informed me.

Once we got our 'donkeys' across the pass, we came to the North Eastern entrance to Yellowstone. We had made it to our destination – the almost mystical Yellowstone National Park!

Once in Yellowstone, we were awestruck by the natural beauty all around us. It was so different from anything that I've seen in my life. It was as if I stepped onto another planet, a planet drenched in beauty. Photographs I had seen of the park simply did not do it justice.

There was glistening snow on the ground near steaming hot pools of water that looked like melted emeralds, or sapphires, or yellow citrines, or a combination of them all. They could have been the source of all the world's jewels in some fairytale. The hot springs had names such as Emerald, Sapphire, Grand Prismatic, and Abyss.

I pictured Native Americans gathered around the steaming pools in order to survive the bitterly cold winters.

Moose, antelope, and elk roamed freely through the park. So did bison and numerous other animals. I so wished every American could visit Yellowstone. So many Americans only see cities or towns and lots of concrete and asphalt and man-made structures. That is not the only America. America is *truly beautiful,* truly stunning, and truly awe-inspiring.

After Linda and I left Yellowstone, we headed to Billings, where I was to spend the night, before jump seating out of Great Falls.

That was our plan anyway. However, Linda and I are explorers at heart, and we rarely travel from point 'A' directly to point 'B.' So it was on this trip that, when we saw a sign for 'Chico Hot Springs,' off we went in that direction.

We soon pulled up to a large lodge, and parked next to a FedEx van that was just pulling away. I smiled and gave a quick wave to the driver. It felt good to know that FedEx had a presence even here, in this off-the-beaten-track little resort. Linda and I walked into the lodge where I picked up a flyer. I read a little about the history of the town.

Apparently, the name Chico was the name of a Mexican man who was so popular with the locals, that, when the area got a Post Office, they officially named the town Chico Hot Springs.

Miners built a wooden structure over one of the hot springs as relief from the cold in the winter. Later, in 1900, a large lodge was built, which enclosed a large hot spring. The lodge and hot spring were a very popular get-a-way for movie stars.

There was a picture on the wall in the lodge lobby of Douglas Fairbanks standing by the indoor hot spring. There was also a plaque advertising a Five-star restaurant on the premises.

'This place was looking better all the time.' I thought. Linda asked the front desk clerk if we could check out one of the rooms. He explained that some of the rooms shared a bath in the hallway, and some had en suite bathrooms. He gave us a key to the latter type of room. The room was on the outside of the lodge and easy to see. We walked up to the door, and let ourselves in.

The room was definitely small. There were two antique iron beds in the room and notably no telephone nor television. I guessed that it had changed little since the place opened in 1900. I pictured how nice it would be to shut out the world and just relax in that room with no intrusion from the outside world. We made a mental note to come back someday to this wonderful little place.

Back in Billings, we spent the night at Linda's house. The next day, she drove me to the airport at Great Falls so that I could catch the Jump Seat back to Memphis.

The airport at Great Falls boasts a very large collection of model airplanes which the airport acquired when someone donated their personal collection. I spent a good half hour or so looking at all of the planes and helicopters on display, prior to heading to the FedEx ramp.

It was still daylight when I boarded the FedEx 727, and I had a good view as I looked out of the cockpit window during take-off.

Unbeknownst to me the Great Falls airport is on a plateau. Thus, when the jet took off, just past the end of the runway, the land dropped off sharply. I was a little surprised to see that as it gave the illusion that the jet had unexpectedly risen dramatically. It took me a second to realize what had happened. I'm just telling you this in order to give you a head's up if you ever fly out of Great Falls.

Anyway that trip to Great Falls was one of my favorite trips as it allowed me to see some of the most beautiful sights in America.

Another trip that we took on a FedEx jet that offered beautiful sights was our trip to Puerto Rico.

Freight is carried to Puerto Rico on a DC-10. In a DC-10 there are jump seats in the cockpit and also two jump seats just outside of the cockpit. Linda and I sat in the jump seats that were outside of the cockpit. When the DC-10 took off, it practically leapt off of the runway at a steep angle.

Since Linda and I were strapped in seats which faced the rear of the plane, we dangled from our seatbelts momentarily, laughing and throwing our arms and legs out in front of us to exaggerate the motion. (I think we did the exact same thing on a ride at the Mid-South Fair in Memphis one year.)   Once the jet leveled out, the flight to Puerto Rico, which is a thousand miles east south east of Miami, was easy going.

It was daylight in Puerto Rico when the big DC-10 touched down. Once on terra firma, we stepped out of the plane and into the sauna of San Juan.

We stayed at the El San Juan hotel and explored the island for the two days that we were there.   This trip had to be short, as we wanted to get back to celebrate our mother's birthday, which is a few days after ours. We were able to visit the fort, El Morro, and swim in the ocean, but not much more, before it was time for us to return to the airport to catch our jump seats back to Memphis.

I had bought a bottle of rum to take back home because I like to make Bananas Foster. (Uh huh.) I was surprised that the rum was distilled in Barbados, not Puerto Rico. But it was 'The World's Oldest Rum' so I figured it must be good. I also purchased a container of cut fruit in a grocery store before going to the airport.

Linda and I said 'Adios' to Puerto Rico as we boarded the jet and strapped into our jump seats just outside of the cockpit door. The DC-10 roared out of Puerto Rico and headed northwest. Once the jet leveled off we opened the container of fruit and snacked on the fruit. After we finished eating, we tried to get comfortable in the jump seats. It's hard for me to sleep while sitting up, but, in fiddling with the seats, I discovered that the seat cushions on the jump seats slip off fairly easily.

Linda and I were elated, as we knew it was a long flight back to Memphis, and we needed to get as comfortable as we could. We removed the seat cushions from our jump seats. I placed mine on the cold metal floor in the area just in front of the huge nylon netting that blocks (hopefully) the modules from shifting. Linda put her cushion closer to the jump seats. We each stretched out and got comfortable on our respective cushions for the long flight back to Memphis.

As I lay on the seat cushions with my eyes closed I was aware of the gentle jostling movement of the plane. It would jostle a little forward, then right, then back, then left. It reminded me of a box step in dancing.

134

That trip to Puerto Rico was one of our grandest birthday trips.

As Linda and I approached our 10-year anniversary at FedEx, we began making plans for a combined birthday/anniversary blowout that would be at a destination even farther away than Puerto Rico.

We chose Australia and New Zealand for this big celebration. Linda and I had kept in touch with our high school Physics teacher, Mr. McNeill. Ray McNeill lives in New Zealand with his wife Doreen.

Mr. McNeill is a pragmatic yet elegant Scotsman who smokes cigarettes using a long black cigarette holder. He used to argue with the Math teacher that there were no such things as

UFOs, while the Math teacher would insist that there were as he had seen one. Mr. McNeill never wishes anyone good luck, because he thinks people should make their own luck.

His wife Doreen is a world renowned artist whose paintings have been exhibited to great acclaim. Some of her paintings hang in the VIP Lounge for Cathay Pacific Airlines in Hong Kong, as well as in many private homes.

Although we still exchange Christmas cards and emails, we wanted to visit the McNeill's in person. Linda and I planned to catch a FedEx 747 with 19 jump seats to take us to our Australian/New Zealand adventure.

But our best laid plans didn't work out. . .

Chapter 13

SO LONG . . .

After eleven years at FedEx, my career was progressing nicely. I had taken business classes at night, and a manager had mentored me into the management program. Before I completed the work to become eligible to apply for management positions, a wrench was thrown into my plans. My husband was unexpectedly transferred by his job from Memphis to a city in another state. I turned in my resignation and left Memphis, before making the trip to Australia or becoming a FedEx manager. But I always heard its best to leave on a high note, and I did.

I keep in touch with some of the friends I made while working at FedEx. I still exchange Christmas cards with several of the friends I made, including one I'll call 'H.' H was my coworker and friend in Flight Training.

H is a talented watercolor artist who paints orchids. She even wrote an article about her love of painting orchids which was published in an Australian orchid magazine. She knows her flowers. When I left Flight Training for job in a department that was half the driving distance to my home, a bouquet of exotic tropical flowers from H arrived at my new desk. Leave it to H to choose such beautiful flowers. The card on the bouquet read, 'Brenda, Happy Landings! May all of your adventures lead you in marvelous directions. I've loved working with you. Love, H.'

I keep H's card inside a book I bought when I first began working for FedEx. The book captured my view of FedEx then, and does 'til this day. It's aptly titled, 'LIVING THE DREAM.' I have had many friends sign it. I hope to have Mr. Smith sign it. And, speaking of Mr. Smith, before I end this, if I may, I have a message for him.

I know you have heard this many times from employees, but I just have to say, "Thank you," for never giving up when you were confronted with so many obstacles on your way to creating Federal Express. Your toughness and tenacity has allowed me and many others to live the dream you dreamed.

Wink.

It's been over twenty-five years since I flew jump seat the first time. Now that I have seen how fast the years fly, I have an even greater appreciation of my years at FedEx, and the memories they provided.

Note: All names have been made up (except for Fred Smith) or initialized in this story.

www.ingramcontent.com/pod-product-compliance
Lightning Source LLC
Chambersburg PA
CBHW061950070426
42450CB00007BA/1179